RED
SQUIRRELS

First published in Great Britain in 1997 by
Colin Baxter Photography Ltd.,
Grantown-on-Spey,
Moray PH26 3NA
Scotland
www.worldlifelibrary.co.uk

Reprinted 1998, 2001, 2005

A CIP Catalogue record for this book is available from the British Library

ISBN 1-900455-24-2

Printed in China

RED SQUIRRELS

Tom Tew & Niall Benvie

Colin Baxter Photography, Grantown-on-Spey, Scotland

Contents

Red Squirrels

The wonderful sight of a British red squirrel high in the treetops is becoming increasingly rare. Sadly, many people, particularly those living in England, will never see a red squirrel. Instead, most people nowadays see only grey squirrels, American cousins of our red squirrel, and are aware that red squirrels are declining and endangered.

Such sentiments would have amazed our ancestors, even as recently as 100 years ago, to whom red squirrels were as common a part of the natural landscape as rabbits or foxes. So what has gone wrong for the red squirrel and what can we do to save it?

The scientific name for the red squirrel is *Sciurus vulgaris*, and this gives a clue both to its demeanour and its former status. The generic term *Sciurus* covers eight different species of northern hemisphere tree squirrel and comes from two Greek words, *skia* meaning 'shadow' and *oura* meaning 'tail'. Thus, *Sciurus* translates as 'an animal sitting in the shadow of its tail' – a rather nice, and accurate, description of tree squirrels. The specific term *vulgaris* is not a derogatory reference to the squirrel's bright red coat, but instead translates as 'common'.

In other words, when the scientific term for the red squirrel was decided, by Linnaeus in 1758, the red squirrel was the 'common' squirrel. Even today, the red squirrel has the largest global range of all squirrels, occurring from the Atlantic coast of Portugal in the west, right across Europe and Asia, to the northern islands of Japan in the east. In Britain, as recently as 1900, red squirrels were widespread and abundant. There is not, therefore, anything intrinsic to the red squirrel's biology to make it a particularly scarce animal, as there is, for example, for some of our native predators who are naturally rather sparsely distributed. There is, however, evidence that British red squirrel populations have historically tended to fluctuate.

Historical Distribution and Abundance

Information on distribution and abundance of the red squirrel is patchy because our predecessors made little attempt to census animals that they considered to be common (a lesson that nature conservationists are only slowly learning to this day). Nevertheless, scattered in the Victorian literature there are several references to the red squirrel and from these we can build a fairly reliable picture of events.

There is little doubt that the red squirrel is native to Britain, colonising the British Isles shortly after the last great ice-cap retreated 10,000 years ago. There are few records prior to the nineteenth century, but it does seem that there was a collapse in the population in the late seventeenth century. By the early eighteenth century the red squirrel was apparently extinct in Ireland and southern Scotland, and by the late eighteenth century it was rare in the Scottish Highlands also.

Towards 1800, therefore, naturalists of that time were becoming concerned at the red squirrel's rarity and in the 1780s a 'reintroduction' was carried out to ten sites in Scotland. A few decades later, from about 1815 onwards, similar reintroductions also took place in Ireland. Most of the stock used for these reintroductions probably came from England, although it is difficult to be certain and some animals could certainly have been brought in from the Continent.

Whether these reintroductions were, in themselves, successful or not is uncertain. It is clear, however, that the British red squirrel population in general returned to a period of 'boom' throughout the nineteenth century, probably thanks to two factors. Firstly, there was a period of extensive new woodland planting that provided a great increase in the habitat available to red squirrels. Secondly, Victorian Britain saw widespread and intensive predator control by the nation's many gamekeepers who were often judged by their masters on the number of predatory corpses hanging on their gibbets. Some of these predators were the natural enemies of red squirrels. By the turn of the twentieth century red squirrels were once again abundant across Britain. Indeed, although it may seem incredible today, in 1910 the Cornwall Squirrel Shooting Club was set up to control the large numbers of red squirrels that were damaging both trees and garden produce. The early years of the twentieth century were, with hindsight, the last golden years for red squirrels in Britain. In 1920 another decline started from which red squirrels have never recovered. The very last wild red squirrels in London, for instance, were seen in Regent's Park in 1942.

The lack of recovery by the red squirrels was down to a man-induced catastrophe. Apparently dissatisfied with the complement of native animals and plants of Britain, the Victorians consistently introduced rare or 'exotic' animals into this country. In those days, they had little idea of what are now accepted ecological concepts concerning niches (gaps in the ecological market place that animals have evolved to exploit) and competition for niches between species. In the last two decades of the nineteenth century and the first two decades of the twentieth, North American grey squirrels (along with other animals such as Chinese muntjac deer) were repeatedly introduced into Britain. By 1920 grey squirrels had established a strong foothold, and between 1930 and 1945 their population exploded – with disastrous consequences for the red squirrel.

Subsequently, suspicion that the grey squirrel might be responsible for the disappearance of the red squirrel arose when the red squirrel's range contraction was closely mirrored by the expanding grey squirrel population. At a national level, therefore, it appeared that red and grey squirrels could not co-exist. Locally, this was noticed throughout the country by people realising

Pure British or with a dash of European blood? We don't yet know the answer.

Now considered both beautiful and rare,
less than a hundred years ago red squirrels were shot as pests.

that red squirrels disappeared a few years after they first saw the invading grey squirrels in their area.

At the start of the twenty-first century, red squirrels have more or less disappeared from England and Wales. There are a few exceptions: island populations on the Isle of Wight, Brownsea and Anglesey; and small vulnerable populations in Thetford and Cannock forests. Apart from this, the only areas where red squirrels are found are the large coniferous forests in North Wales and remaining outposts in north-west (Cumbria) and north-east (Northumbria) England. Every month, local red squirrel groups report the further spread of the grey squirrel into these areas and the outlook for the British red squirrel south of Scotland appears gloomy.

The historical fact that red squirrel populations fluctuated widely has led some people to assert that the introduction of the grey squirrel is not a causal factor behind the decline of the red, but merely a historical coincidence. Can we be absolutely certain that the grey squirrel is to blame?

The short scientific answer is 'no'; to obtain a scientific 'yes' would mean setting up large-scale and expensive field experiments, which would need to run over several decades. Red squirrel conservationists argue that we cannot afford the time to wait for such results, even if these experiments were ethically acceptable. Furthermore, the vast majority of conservationists are already convinced that the main factor behind the current disappearance of the red squirrel is the grey squirrel – the historical evidence is simply too strong to ignore. Disease, weather and habitat loss have all played their part, but in the absence of grey squirrels it is thought that the red squirrel would by now have bounced back to its former common status. Red squirrel populations have probably always tended to fluctuate – it is an innate consequence of their biology and ecology – but the introduction of an alien competitor into Britain, at a time when the red squirrel populations were naturally low, drove a nail into the coffin.

Biology and Ecology

Squirrels are rodents, and rodents in general are so successful that they comprise 40% of all the mammal species in the world. Partly, this success stems from the fact that they are, evolutionarily speaking, a very young group (about 30 million years old). This means that there is a large amount of genetic variability in the group. Coupled with the fact that they are rapid breeders, this makes the rodents a very adaptable evolutionary force. Furthermore, rodents have very efficient gnawing front teeth (the Latin word *rodere* means 'to gnaw') and grinding cheek teeth, which allows them a varied and wide-ranging diet. This allows rodents to be personally, as well as evolutionarily, highly adaptable and opportunistic. Rats and mice are the most famous rodents, but squirrels are close cousins and share many of their traits. There are three sub-orders of rodents – mice, porcupines and squirrels – and in the squirrel sub-order alone there are 365 different species in seven families.

Even though they are now rare in Britain, most people would recognise a red squirrel if they saw one. They are beautiful and photogenic animals, attributes that keep them on Christmas cards and in the public's eye even if, nowadays, children's books use grey squirrels rather than the red squirrels that starred in their parents' or grand-parents' early reading matter ('Spot the Dog', circa 1990, is friends with a grey squirrel, while 'Rupert the Bear', circa 1950, always spoke to red squirrels!).

Male and female red squirrels are very similar to look at, and coat colour is no clue because this varies considerably. Also, individuals change their coat with the seasons. In winter, red squirrels have a thick warm coat, usually of deep red, and impressive red ear tufts some 1¼ in (3 cm) long; the tail is thick, bushy and dark red – the most impressively beautiful squirrels are those in their winter finery. In summer, looks are sacrificed for a thinner, more pragmatic coat; often lighter in colour, more of a chestnut hue, with a thinner tail.

A red squirrel's body is about 8½ in (22 cm) long, with the tail almost as long again; in this respect, they are not much smaller than the grey squirrel, which measures 10 in (26 cm) nose to tail-base. However, adult red squirrels are surprisingly light for their size, only weighing, on average, about 10½ oz (300 gm), whereas grey squirrels, at 19 oz (550 gm), are nearly twice as heavy.

Red squirrels have pretty good eyesight and a wide field of view, important for spotting potential predators. They appear to have dichromatic vision, which means that they can differentiate red from blue but not red from green, so they see like a red-green colour blind human does. They also have a very sensitive cat-like set of whiskers with which they can judge distance and size.

All squirrels have five digits front and back, although the thumbs are very small and it looks as though they only have four fingers. Both fingers and toes have long and strong claws which are essential for climbing and the front hands are very dextrous at handling and manipulating small objects like seeds. Red squirrels appear, like humans, to be either right- or left-handed.

It is not known how long red squirrels can live in the wild: it is likely to be about six or seven years at the maximum, although in captivity they have reached the age of ten.

The characteristic bushy tail is mainly used for balance, but may also be employed as a signalling tool. Many people will have seen 'angry' squirrels chittering their displeasure and flicking their tail in apparent annoyance. In gardens this is often directed at the local cat, but the tail is most frequently and importantly used in communicating with friends and enemies, rivals and potential mates, of their own species. Bushy tails may also be important in keeping warm, particularly over winter, and, on the whole, a squirrel that loses or damages its tail, which sometimes happens as a result of encounters with predators or motor cars, will struggle to survive.

Dextrous hands and teeth skilfully manipulate food items.

Although happiest in a tree, squirrels
will often venture onto the ground and are quick and nimble.

For most of the time, red squirrels are fairly solitary, although there are obviously exceptions during the breeding season at the start of the calendar year, when the rough and tumble of finding and keeping a mate often results in highly vocal and visible games of chase among the treetops. There are also records of communal nesting by red squirrels, especially during the cold winter weather and probably among family members or known neighbours.

Red squirrels have 'home ranges', which means that they have a set area through which they will travel regularly and know well. They will not, however, fight each other over these areas of woodland, except in certain circumstances such as a mother protecting an area for her young litter. Home range sizes are variable but, on average, are about 17½ acres (7 ha). Home ranges of different animals will overlap, and red squirrel densities are normally between 0.3 and 1 animal per 2½ acres (1 ha), irrespective of the type of woodland. By comparison, grey squirrel densities are, like red squirrels, up to 1 per hectare in coniferous woodland, but in deciduous woodland can often be up to 3 animals per acre (8 per hectare).

Red squirrels have two basic types of nest, called dreys, a robust winter version and a more temporary summer home. The summer home is really just a resting platform for when the weather is hot or for a brief night's sleep. It is usually a rather hastily constructed platform of twigs, and often doesn't last very long. The winter drey, on the other hand, is a substantial home: dreys can reach 20 in (50 cm) in diameter and last for several years before falling down. The winter drey must last the squirrel as a refuge right through the bitter weather and strong winds and be both weatherproof and predator-proof. It comprises two layers: on the outside a thick layer of interwoven twigs (normally taken from the tree in which the drey is situated), and on the inside a warm and comfortable layer of moss, leaves and fur. In the case of females, where these dreys are used for raising the young, the inside layer will be made particularly cosy. Apart from the breeding drey, red squirrels are prone to building and using more than one drey in their home range, and often two or three dreys will be in concurrent use. As mentioned previously, sometimes winter dreys are shared with friends and family, especially if the weather is cold.

In general, dreys are built more than 10 ft (3 m) off the ground. They won't be too high, or too exposed, however, since protection from the wind is important, normally below 30 ft (9 m) and often close to the main trunk. Also, the drey will usually be built in a tree within a clump of trees; a good selection of nearby trees offers more avenues of escape in emergencies. A good time to look out for squirrel dreys is during the autumn when the leaves first fall; during the summer the dreys are well camouflaged and difficult to spot.

Breeding Biology

The breeding biology of the red squirrel is fairly straightforward but breeding success is heavily dependent on the amount of food available. Both male and female red squirrels are promiscuous – males will mate with more than one female and females with more than one male. Mating occurs without any courtship to speak of, apart from a 'mating chase' in which a female in oestrus is chased amongst the treetops by a gaggle of males. Their urgency stems from the fact that the female is in heat for just one day each cycle, but during this day her odour will attract all the neighbouring males. The females' normally aggressive attitude to males is softened somewhat during this period, probably helped by the variety of soothing appeasement calls made by the males. During the chase the dominance hierachy of males becomes clear. Dominance is probably related to age, weight and experience, but may also be influenced by the proximity of the males' and females' ranges. Once mating has occurred, the male considers his parental duties to be fulfilled, and will contribute

When the weather is cold, red squirrels quickly lose heat once they leave their nests.

The foraging squirrel faces very hard choices in the winter.

nothing further to the rearing and development of his offspring.

The breeding season can start as early as December, as the young adults born the previous year start to mate, and go on till September, when the summer litters are weaned. There are two peaks in the numbers of young born, the first around March and the second in June. In an average year, pregnancy will last 5–6 weeks, with an average of three young per litter, who will be suckled for between 8 and 10 weeks. Thus, most adult females will only raise one litter of young per year. However, in very good years when the weather is mild and food is plentiful, quite a few females will squeeze in a second litter, a lot more females in total will breed, the number of young born per litter will rise, and the survival rate through to weaning will rise. Red squirrels can therefore take advantage of good years when they occur, and the number of juvenile squirrels about in the autumn is highly dependent on the food supply of that year.

Red squirrels weigh only about 0.3–0.5 oz (10–15 g) when they are born and are hairless, blind, deaf and unable to clean themselves. Their mother is fiercely protective of them for the next two months. Their hair starts to grow after one or two weeks and their lower and upper incisors are cut at about three and five weeks respectively. Their ears and eyes do not open until they are about a month old and it is not until they are about seven weeks old that they start to take solid food and are able to dig and climb well.

After two months the youngsters start to leave the nest and explore, initially under the watchful eye of their mother, who will retrieve them by the scruff of the neck if she feels they have strayed too far. Gradually, the maternal ties are loosened and the youngsters stray further from the nest and start staying away altogether. When the family is raised mid-season the mother will often tolerate her offspring for the entire autumn and winter, before turfing them out of her home range into the wide world. When the litter is an early one, however, the youngsters will be driven away by their mother during the summer as she comes into oestrus for her second litter of the year.

Activity and Feeding

Contrary to popular belief, red squirrels do not hibernate, although they do become less active over the winter. Squirrels are always active during the day, although the timing of their activity varies over the year. In winter they tend to come out in late morning and forage during the middle of the short day. In summer, when days are much longer and warmer, squirrels show two bursts of activity: for a couple of hours after dawn and then again for a couple of hours before dusk. These, obviously, are the coolest parts of the day. The squirrel seems to be for ever trying to keep its body temperature reasonable, and this is a characteristic of many small warm-blooded animals who lose and gain heat rather more rapidly than larger animals of the same design. For squirrels, therefore, there is a year-long mix of heat and energy conservation during the winter,

Squirrel dreys can be spotted more easily in autumn and winter.

and cooling-off periods during the summer.

In practice, this means that during the winter the individual red squirrel has a very difficult choice to make. Should he leave his warm nest to try and forage? Or should he stay put to try and conserve energy? The choice depends on the weather, and in very cold temperatures, or in strong winds or heavy rain, it is rare to see red squirrels out and about. So much, too, depends

Strong hands and feet and long claws make going down as easy as going up.

24

on the availability of food; if there are plenty of nuts around from the previous autumn then life will be bearable. Indeed, if the weather is mild and the previous autumn was a good nut year, then some red squirrels even start breeding during the winter. But if the weather is harsh, the ground is frozen, and the nut crop failed the previous autumn, then winter is a very difficult time for red squirrels. Animals are forced out of their nest to search for food; as they do so they quickly lose heat, and if they cannot find food they become yet colder and more hungry: a vicious circle is set up and many animals will die.

Both red and grey squirrels are tree-dwelling forest animals. There is a temptation to think of grey squirrels as inhabitants of deciduous woodland and red squirrels as pine forest creatures but this is not strictly true. The natural forest of Britain is a mix of broad-leaved trees such as oak, ash, elm, beech and chestnut, often with an understorey of hazelnut. Before the grey squirrel arrived in Britain, the red squirrel was spread right across the country; equally, red squirrels are found across continental Europe and Asia in natural forests of broad-leaved tree species, although the dominant tree species across their world range are coniferous. Thus we can say that although red squirrels have evolved largely in coniferous forests they are also, if left to their own devices, quite happy living in natural broad-leaved woodland.

Like most rodents, squirrels in general are not fussy eaters and the red squirrel is no exception; that is not to say, however, that food is unimportant or always easy to find, rather the reverse is true and food availability is one of the keys to the survival of the red squirrel. In broad terms squirrels are vegetarians and will eat most of whatever is going. Undoubtedly, their main foodstuff is tree seeds (nuts), but they will also eat berries and fungi when these are available. It often surprises people that red squirrels like fungi, but in one study on the Isle of Wight the red squirrels spent 90% of their active time

Even when feeding, vigilance against predators must be maintained at all times.

during the month of December eating a certain type of fungus that grew on the oak trees. Other food items include shoots and buds, flowers and bark, and lichens. Occasionally, they will also stray from vegetarianism and eat insects and birds' eggs.

Feeding signs are quite easy to spot. Larger nuts such as hazels are split in two, with the pieces of shell showing clean edges, rather than the gnawing marks of smaller woodland rodents such as mice and voles. Also characteristic are the discarded cores of eaten fir cones, which are generally neater when left by squirrels than when left by seed-eating birds. Squirrels will often eat at a favoured site, and a tree-stump surrounded by these discarded cones is a good field-sign of squirrels. Feeding on bark is quite easy to spot, since the bark often hangs down in long spiral strips; this can be at any height, from base to treetop. All in all, the red squirrel has a catholic diet, but food availability is the key.

One way to get around the problems of great changes in food availability is to stock your larder. In other words, when times are good and food is plentiful, it makes sense for the individual squirrel to set up a private hoard of food that only he knows about, and to which he can return in times of hardship. The problem is that there will be others around who would like to raid that store, both fellow squirrels and other birds and animals too. Red squirrels store two types of food: fungi and seeds. Fungi are simply jammed into nooks and crannies where they dry out and remain edible for long periods. Seeds and cones are buried singly at wide intervals throughout the home range. In one study of squirrels that was done in Belgium this has particularly been observed of red squirrels caching Scots pine cones in the autumn, presumably to deny access to birds who would, if the cones were left on the ends of the branches, have constant access throughout the winter. It is not known whether squirrels actually remember individual locations or just a general area; many people will have seen squirrels frantically scrabbling about an area looking for

Remembering where nuts were buried can prove vital.

a previously buried nut, and this *modus operandi* tends to suggest the latter tactic. However, it has been shown that adult red squirrels can smell and find pine cones that have been buried 12 in (30 cm) underground, and there is a good chance that searching may reveal someone else's buried larder. Incidentally, this squirrel-mediated dispersal is undoubtedly a very convenient and effective method for a new tree to start its life – assuming the squirrel forgets where it buried the nut!

Red squirrels are much happier, and safer, in the tree canopy than on the ground, and appear to spend about 70% of their time off the ground. Nevertheless, when on the ground they are fleet of foot and scurry or leap in a series of agile bounds; frequent pauses to check for danger, with head and tail up, characterise their distinctive and much-loved posture. Red squirrels can also swim, although this is a matter of having to in an emergency rather than choosing to. High in the tree canopy, their agility and jumping prowess make them formidably quick and they have a variety of 'escape' behaviour, including climbing up the 'blind' side of tree trunks and branches or, sometimes, 'freezing' with the body and tail pressed down flat against the trunk or branch. While such behaviour makes them a difficult prey, they are not entirely immune from attack.

Red squirrels are occasionally taken by a wide variety of predators but their speed and agility means that there are only a couple of squirrel 'specialists' in Britain – goshawks and pine martens. Even when such predators are naturally distributed, they would take only a very small proportion of the squirrel population. In modern-day Britain, where both goshawks and pine martens have suffered from human persecution (there are currently fewer than 1000 goshawks and 4000 pine martens in Britain), there is very little chance of these animals having a significant effect on the red squirrel population.

An individual squirrel will know all the safest places in its home range to sit and eat.

Conservation

We have seen how red squirrel populations in Britain appear to have fluctuated over the past few hundred years, and it has been noted that the current drastic decline in red squirrel numbers seems to be linked to the introduction of the North American grey squirrel. How is it that one species can drive out another and what, if anything, can we do about it?

The red squirrel is now essentially restricted to Scotland and northern England, with small isolated populations scattered elsewhere, including a few large coniferous forests in the English Midlands, East Anglia, the Welsh mountains, and some healthy populations on a few isolated islands, particularly the Isle of Wight. It is still widespread throughout Ireland, although a decline in distribution may now be occurring in Northern Ireland. It was estimated in 1995 that there were only 160,000 red squirrels in Britain, with 120,000 in Scotland, 30,000 in England and 10,000 in Wales; of the English squirrels, roughly 85% were in Cumbria and Northumbria. Although there have been no complete resurveys since then, the range of red squirrels continues to contract, and numbers presumably continue to fall. Conversely, it is estimated that there are over 2.5 million grey squirrels in Britain.

Scientific research suggests that the grey squirrel exerts what ecologists call 'competitive diet exclusion' (see below) over the red squirrel, because it has evolved to be better-placed than the red squirrel in deciduous woodland.

The respective weight of the two species is a crucial point. Grey squirrels, at about 19 oz (550 gm), are approximately twice the weight of red squirrels. This difference in weight has risen over time as the two species have evolved different feeding strategies. The two species did not evolve side-by-side; the grey squirrel has only very recently been introduced by man as a competitor to the red squirrel. The larger grey squirrels hold a significant advantage over the smaller reds. The red squirrel has evolved to be a more arboreal and specialised animal than the grey squirrel, spending far more of its time foraging high up in the trees. With its agility and lightness – it can climb the thinnest twig and feed on the smallest seeds such as those of conifers, which are extracted one-by-one from pine cones – the red squirrel is a skilled and delicate eater. The heavier, more robust grey squirrel is less delicate. The great advantage it has over the red squirrel, which allows it to be bigger, appears to be in its digestive physiology with respect to the large seeds such as chestnut, hazelnut and acorn. Crucially, in deciduous woodland, grey squirrels are physiologically not only better able to more efficiently use, i.e. digest, some of the available seed crop (particularly acorns), but can also eat part of the seed crop (particularly hazelnuts) before it fully ripens and, therefore, before red squirrels can.

Where the two species overlap, in broad-leaved woodland, competition between the two is therefore a bit one-sided, because the grey squirrels can eat most of the seed crop before the red squirrels get so much as a sniff and, even where red squirrels do get a chance to eat the acorns, they are of less nutritional benefit to them than they are to the grey squirrels.

The unequal competition between the two species is further exacerbated by their differences in size and the need they have to put on weight to allow them to overwinter successfully. When the weather is hard and foraging is ruled out, it pays to have a nice fat body to keep you warm and plenty of fat reserves to keep you going with energy. However, red squirrels have evolved to be small and nimble foragers; they can't afford to put on too much weight in the autumn and, on average, probably increase their bodyweight by about 10% (about 1 oz/30 gm). The heavyweight greys don't have to be too fussy about their weight and put on about 20% in body weight (about 4 oz/110 gm) during the autumn. Thus, the grey squirrels can store 3–4 times as much fat as red squirrels, and in British deciduous woodland with a mix of hazelnut and

When it comes to food, red squirrels invariably lose out in competition with grey squirrels.

oaks, the red squirrels naturally would rely heavily upon hazelnut availability to put on fat in the autumn, and store some hazelnuts in their larders, and so maintain their weight and health throughout the winter. When grey squirrels are abundant (and once established they quickly become so because their populations are boosted by the presence of oak trees with their supply of acorns), they eat all the hazelnuts first, before the red squirrels have a chance. The reduction in available hazelnuts for the reds results in weight loss which leads to reduced overwintering success and reduced breeding success.

Is there any hope for the red squirrel? Without human intervention, the situation in deciduous woodland appears bleak, although there may be steps that can be taken, which are discussed later. In some coniferous forests, however, red squirrels appear to be able to outcompete grey squirrels. Scientists aren't yet sure exactly what sort of forests will be best in all circumstances, and the situation may not be the same throughout Britain, but research from Wales by squirrel conservationists and foresters suggests that in large areas (in excess of 5000 acres/2000 ha) of conifer-dominated forest there may be hope. Suitable conifer forests should have 'buffer zones' of conifer trees or open land of at least 2 miles (3 km) to stop grey squirrels spreading into the red squirrel reserve. For the same reason, there should be a low ratio of boundary length to wood area – circular or square forests are better than long thin strips of forest. There should also be high 'connectivity' for red squirrels between seed-producing areas, so no large woodland rides or open areas that would tend to isolate red squirrel individuals or populations. In terms of tree type, there should be a three-way split between young (less than 15 years), medium (15–30 years) and old (more than 30 years) trees and a suitable species composition; Scots and lodgepole pine, spruce, firs, yew, hawthorn and rose are all thought to favour red squirrels, while birch, rowan, ash, willow,

On mainland Britain, the only place to get this view is in a large coniferous forest.

aspen and alder are thought to be 'neutral'. Management of the wood should include the sparing of single and clumped trees to provide nesting sites. Perhaps recommendations such as these will mean that woodland managers of the future, particularly of the conifer-dominated commercial forestry industry, will be able to help conserve the red squirrel in large parts of Britain.

Unfortunately, other studies in the south of England have proved less encouraging for red squirrel conservationists. In an area of coniferous forest

Larger nuts are split in two, with the shells showing clean edges.

around Poole harbour it was found that red squirrels did not get enough of a competitive advantage over grey squirrels to really thrive. Perhaps red squirrels only have a good enough advantage over grey squirrels in low productivity coniferous forests. The scientists responsible for this work believe that we should look towards 'island' habitats, either literally as in the Isle of Wight, or metaphorically as in an isolated woodland surrounded by a buffer zone, for the future of red squirrel conservation in southern Britain.

A further problem for the red squirrel has arisen as a result of a recent trend to plant deciduous trees within conifer plantations. Such decisions were well-intentioned and were designed to diversify habitat for the wildlife and increase human enjoyment of the conifer plantation by making woodland

The tail is used for balance, it is also a shelter, a signalling device and a body warmer.

walks more varied and interesting. Unfortunately, the introduction of some species of deciduous tree and shrub, especially those with large seeds such as oak, beech, hazel and chestnut, provides an introductory foothold in the wood for grey squirrels and allows corridors for them to invade and penetrate deep into the conifer wood. Similarly, fragmentation of good habitat may also make some areas less suitable for red squirrels, increasing their vulnerability to displacement by grey squirrels. Large, unfragmented blocks of mixed conifer forest are considered the best habitat for red squirrels and these should be preserved wherever possible.

Such management of forests, while extremely desirable, is really part of a long-term goal. There are also practical, and more immediate, although not always palatable, ways that humans can assist the survival of red squirrels. The two main ways are either to drive out or eliminate the alien grey squirrel, or somehow to tip the balance of survival to favour the red squirrel over the grey.

If we concede that the grey squirrel is largely responsible for the decline in the red squirrel (this is now generally accepted, even if not entirely proven) then we must also accept that red squirrels will not be able to occupy their 'natural' range in the UK unless and until grey squirrels are eliminated from the UK. However, the elimination, or even partial control, of a species is neither a simple nor unemotive matter for either conservationists or the general public. Widespread control of the grey squirrel has been tried before, in the 1950s, when the grey squirrel was a 'new' pest species to many country folk. The government of the day offered a bounty for each grey squirrel tail that was handed in to the authorities. Unfortunately, the gamekeepers soon worked out that their best policy was not to kill all the grey squirrels in one go, since this would result in just a single one-off payment, but to 'harvest' the squirrels from a patch, just a few at a time, thus instigating a reliable and consistent

Ears pricked, eyes wide and body hugging the trunk – a predator may be nearby.

source of income. This was 'sustainable use of a natural resource by native peoples' 40 years before the phrase became fashionable amongst conservationists! The bounty system failed to halt the spread of the grey squirrel and was rather expensive, so was soon stopped.

There are now new ways of ensuring that only grey squirrels are targeted in any control campaign, which involve very selective and targeted delivery mechanisms for anti-coagulents, which work on grey squirrels as rat poison does on rats. Not unnaturally, the use of such techniques is opposed by many (although they do not have such sympathy for rats). Scientists are now looking at a new generation of control agents such as immuno-contraceptives. If such work proceeds to plan, grey squirrels might be entirely painlessly neutered, and the population would die out without causing any animal suffering. There is still a long way to go before such techniques are ready to be used in the field and it is clearly crucial that the technique is 100% foolproof before it can be used.

Equally importantly, many people (particularly, perhaps, those living in cities) have grown to love and value the grey squirrel as a significant part of their surroundings. It does not really matter to them that the grey squirrel is an 'alien' species introduced from elsewhere, nor do they care that grey squirrels may cause serious economic damage to forestry interests. Many conservationists accept that, currently at least, the majority of the British public would not wish to be entirely rid of the grey squirrel, even if it were possible.

Given that this is so, it follows that we must also accept that the red squirrel will never return to its full natural range in the UK, and that there are large parts of the country where red squirrels can no longer occur unless a high level of human intervention is maintained indefinitely. There will be some areas – the last outposts of the red squirrel in England, for instance – where targeted direct action may be desirable, and it is in these areas that control of grey squirrels may be feasible. A large-scale trial of such a programme is being

Just like grey squirrels (and pheasants!),
red squirrels will happily take advantage of human kindness.

conducted on the island of Anglesey, off the Welsh mainland; control of grey squirrels here seems to be having a very positive effect, and early reports suggest that 2004 was the best breeding season for red squirrels for many years, with over 500 young born. Even outside such trial areas, however, especial care should be taken to prevent the spread of the grey squirrel into those areas where currently the red squirrel population is isolated, e.g. islands (either offshore or isolated mainland habitats).

Another way of helping the red squirrel is to provide food for the red squirrels but not for the grey squirrels. Field researchers have designed a clever food 'hopper' that can do this, which works by using the difference in weight between the two species. A trip-door mechanism lies between the food and the tunnel entrance and only light squirrels can get past it; thus, red squirrels have access to a big, dry and ripe pile of nuts, while the heavier grey squirrels fall out of the bottom of the tunnel on their way to the pile. By deploying these feeding hoppers, it is hoped that red squirrels can gather enough food to put on sufficient weight to overwinter and breed successfully, even in the face of opposition from the grey squirrels.

Where artificial feeding is widespread, such as at Formby on the Lancashire coast, there do indeed seem to be more red squirrels about than in conditions where red and grey squirrels are competing. It is not yet clear if this is a general rule that might be applied elsewhere, and other studies have either failed to detect any beneficial effect or have demonstrated the ephemeral nature of such effects. Conservationists are also worried about the potential problems that the artificial feeding of wild animals may cause, such as bringing together lots of wild animals into an unnaturally small area (with perhaps an increase in the risks of disease and predation), or encouraging red squirrels to cache unnaturally large amounts of food which are then

Red squirrels do not hibernate and are out and about all year long.

found and used by grey squirrels. For supplemental feeding to be successful it should be consistent and long-term, perhaps even indefinite; it is pointless, perhaps even counter-productive and cruel, to build up a red squirrel population by artificial feeding and then withdraw that feeding, and so supplemented feeding must be seen as a major commitment. In general terms, the supplementary feeding of red squirrels requires careful planning to consider exactly how it might affect red squirrels, careful targeting to ensure that it is only used in those areas of the country that will benefit, and especially careful monitoring over specified time periods to measure the effects that it has had on the red squirrel.

For the conservation of red squirrels to be successful, a co-ordinated effort across Britain is desirable. Such co-ordination began with the publication of the *UK Strategy for Red Squirrel Conservation*, by the Joint Nature Conservation Committee, who are Government advisors on nature conservation. The *UK Strategy* has the support of all squirrel conservationists, the main aim being to maintain healthy and self-sustaining populations of red squirrels in areas where grey squirrels are rare or absent.

The *UK Strategy* sets out mechanisms to achieve these aims, including the monitoring of red squirrel populations by recording their numbers and distribution across the country, good management of the habitat or resources to try and tip the balance away from the grey squirrel and in favour of the red squirrel, scientific research to improve knowledge of the ecology of red squirrels so that we can better help them in the future, and the promotion of their status and needs to as wide an audience as possible, so that people realise just how endangered the red squirrel has become.

The last native terrestrial mammal to go extinct in Britain was the wolf in the mid eighteenth century; we must hope that the red squirrel is not the next, and that our children and grandchildren will still have the opportunity to see these beautiful animals in the woods of Britain.

Red Squirrel Facts

Scientific name:		*Sciurus vulgaris*
Other names:		common squirrel, brown squirrel, con, skug
Size:		head and body 8½ in (22 cm)
Weight:		10½ oz (300 g) on average when adult
Habitat:		found in woodland of all types and in urban areas on the Continent
Breeding:		pregnancy 5–6 weeks, average litter size of 3, lactation 8–10 weeks
Diet:		mainly seeds but will take a wide variety of other foods, including fungi, fruits, berries, buds, shoots and flowers
Signs:	Footprints	four toes on forefeet showing, pointing forwards, five toes on hindfeet
	Tracks	characteristic with forefeet behind and inside line of larger hindfeet, stride about 13¾ in (35 cm)
	Faeces	cylindrical or round, colour depending on diet, slightly smaller than those of rabbit
	Feeding	hazelnuts split open leaving two pieces of shell with clean edges, characteristic cones of conifer with associated piles of stripped scales; remains scattered but sometimes clumped on or around tree stumps

Recommended Reading

The best all-round book is *The Natural History of Squirrels* by John Gurnell (Christopher Helm, London, 1987) which is packed with scientific facts but very readable. For a good, short, scientific summary see the relevant section in *The Handbook of British Mammals* edited by Gordon Corbet and Stephen Harris (Blackwell, Oxford, 1991). For a wider look at squirrels of the world see the relevant section in *The Encyclopaedia of Mammals* by David Macdonald (Unwin, London, 1984).

The *UK Strategy for Red Squirrel Conservation* was published in 1996 by the Joint Nature Conservation Committee, Peterborough, and is available from them free of charge upon request.

Biographical Note

Tom Tew's boyhood interest in wildlife culminated in a Ph.D. at Oxford University as part of the Wildlife Conservation Research Unit. Tom became a Senior Vertebrate Ecologist in the UK Joint Nature Conservation Committee, and edited the contributions of British red squirrel conservationists, and wildlife, landowning and forestry organisations, into the *UK Strategy for Red Squirrel Conservation*. He is now a Regional Director for English Nature.

Niall Benvie is a Scottish photographer who specialises in the wildlife and wild land of his home country. His work is widely published and has appeared in other books in the WorldLife Library series.